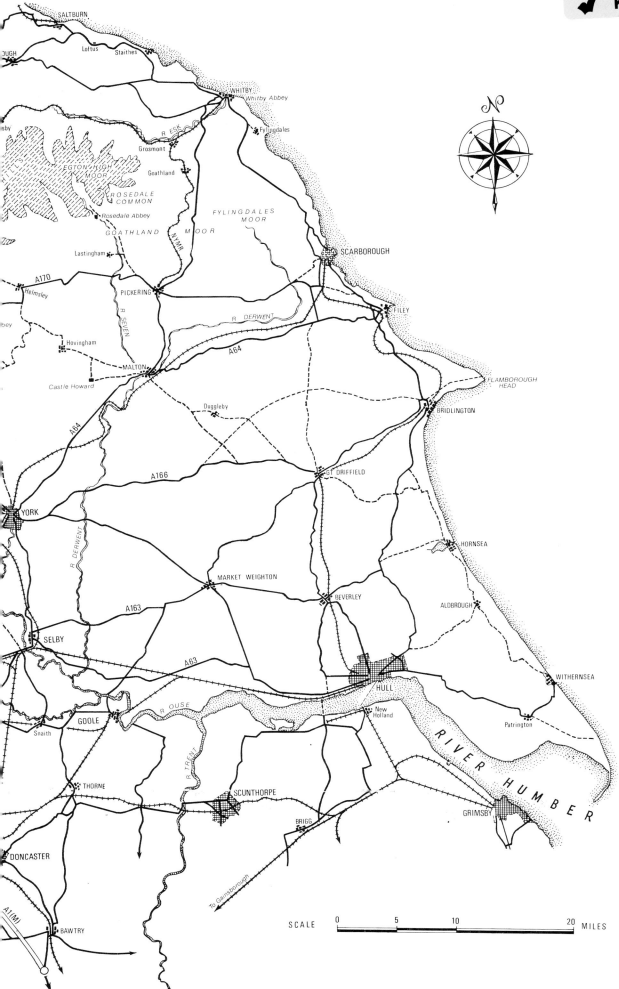

SCALE 0 5 10 20 MILES

England in cameracolour
Yorkshire

England in cameracolour
Yorkshire

Photographs by F. A. H. BLOEMENDAL

Text by ALAN HOLLINGSWORTH

LONDON

IAN ALLAN LTD

First published 1980
Reprinted 1981

ISBN 0 7110 1031 5

Published by Ian Allan Ltd, Shepperton, Surrey,
and printed in Italy by
Graphische Betriebe Athesia, Bolzano

Introduction

The Yorkshire of this book is not the mutilated county of the reviled 1974 Act of Parliament but 'Greater Yorkshire' – the Yorkshire of tradition, of county cricket, of centuries of a common heritage and manner of speech that is essentially English but within England unique. For Yorkshire is now like 'East Anglia', the 'West Country' and the 'Home Counties', an area that defies strict bureaucratic delineation but is nonetheless unmistakeably itself. And quite unmistakeable is the face that Yorkshire presents to the artist's eye whether he uses paint as his medium like Turner who did some of his best work in Wharfedale, or whether like the artist whose work is featured in this book, F.A.H. Bloemendal, he uses a camera.

Greater Yorkshire lies roughly between the Humber in the south and the Tees in the north, from the North Sea coast in the east to the western edge of the Pennine range. Geographically it can be divided into four major regions: the Pennine country which accounts for more than a third of the land area and includes the great industrial powerhouse where the energy is coal and the product is wool in the south, and the Yorkshire Dales National Park in the north; the vast agricultural region of the Vale of York through which flows not only the River Ouse whose tributaries drain almost the entire county but also the major road and rail links that hold the United Kingdom itself together; the tableland of the North Yorkshire Moors, another National Park; and finally, southwards from it across the Vale of Pickering, the Yorkshire Wolds and the crumbling cliffs of the North Sea coast.

At various periods of geological history, the whole of what is now Yorkshire spent millions of years under primeval seas, swamps and rivers. The result is that the bulk of the rocks responsible for the structure of the county and its scenery are of a sedimentary nature, deposits of limestones, sandstones, shales and what the geologists call 'coal measures'. First at the bottom of a shallow sea the shells of primitive crustaceans steadily built a deep layer of limey deposit, then as rivers brought mud into the area shales were built up over the limestone, and finally above the mud, sand flats formed. Primitive tree ferns grew on the sand flats, the sea flowed in and the whole cycle was repeated. In many parts of Pennine Yorkshire the sides of the valleys, with their steep grassy slopes interrupted at intervals like layers in a cake by craggy scars, reveal the history of their own creation (see page 36). The layers are not, however, regular or flat because in nearer geological times the Pennines were created by a massive earth movement that pushed, folded and creased these softer rocks against the older harder rocks to the North. The result is that the Pennines are essentially a giant rounded whaleback fold, or anticlyne, rather higher in the west than in the east. The rest of the shaping has been carried out over the aeons of geological time by the action of the weather – mostly of water in either its liquid form or as ice.

At various comparatively recent geological times the whole of Yorkshire was also under the ice of a great ice cap that extended across Europe and the North Sea from Scandinavia. The last of these 'Ice Ages' – geologists say there were four – ended a mere 10,000 years ago and the glacier spreading south from Scotland was split by the Pennines and the North Yorkshire Moors. One ice front gouged out the northern Vale of York and besides deposits of boulder clay, left heaps of its debris – moraine, they are called – as far south as York and along the edge of the Pennines and the North York Moors. Another limb of the glacier ran down the east coast as far as the Wash but was contained in its westward spread by the Yorkshire and Lincolnshire Wolds. When the ice melted, great lakes formed – Lake Pickering between the Moors and the Wolds, Lake Humber which covered the lower parts of the Vale of York from York down to Grantham, from Leeds to Lincoln Edge. There are still traces of these lakes today in the marshy land around Pickering and south of Goole. And after the ice and the lakes, the rivers carved the rest of the deeper lines on Yorkshire's physical face.

In the Pennines, the presence of workable 'coal measures' south of the 'Aire Gap' provided the fuel for the industrial development of the West Riding. Tilted at a comparatively shallow angle these layers of coal extend eastwards under the Vale of York hence the recent development of an immense new coalfield at Drax south of Selby. But Yorkshire's black-gold triangle – with its points at Keighley, Goole and Sheffield – accounts for less than a quarter of the county's land area. Herein lies the wealth and not a little of the beauty, for industrial Yorkshire is no great flat conurbation like the Midlands but in the windy hills the jet is often happily set among the emeralds of grass, and sometimes among amethysts of heather. South of the 'Aire Gap' – a geological disarrangement known as the Craven fault – we also find millstone grit, a sedimentary sandstone much used for walling, paving and roofing and known generically as 'York Stone'.

The Yorkshire Pennines north of the Aire Valley are known collectively as 'The Dales'. 'Dale' is a word of Scandinavian origin meaning 'valley' and its counterpart is 'fell' which means a large space open to the sky. We have only to add one or two more old Norse words like 'beck' (stream), 'scar' for cliff, 'gill' for ravine and 'side' meaning the slope of a hill, especially one extending for a distance, and 'pot' for cave to have a complete word picture of the Dales as pages 26, 28, 36 will quickly demonstrate. Here limestone is the dominant surface ; rock and heather don't like a limey soil but grass does – hence the green horizons dotted with sheep. The Dales themselves are in fact valleys cut by rivers – occasionally helped by ice action – and the northernmost one is Teesdale. The Tees rises on the slopes of bleak Cross Fell in Cumbria, flows south-east through Barnard Castle, skirts Darlington and enters the North Sea at Middlesbrough. The rest of the major dales' rivers flow south-eastward to sustain the Ouse for the slow journey across the flat Vale of York to the Humber at Goole. Of the five main dales' rivers – the Swale, the Ure that runs through Wensleydale, the Nidd, the Wharfe and the Ribble – all but the Nidd rise on the higher western ridge of the fells and only the Ribble turns westward to flow into the Irish Sea. There are many other named dales just to confuse the visitor but virtually all are tributaries to main ones. The better known ones are Colsterdale and Coverdale on Wensleydale, Littondale on Wharfedale, and Malhamdale which runs into Airedale.

As Herriot fans will know, the Dales provide good grazing for cattle with summer pasture on the upper slopes for sheep. But with the valleys running east and west the land is not suitable for arable farming and ploughed fields are rare.

The North York Moors with the Cleveland Hills to the north-west and the Hambledon Hills to the west, make up Yorkshire's other National Park. They too are made of sedimentary rocks although of a younger, softer type than the Dales with gritty sandstones predominating. The hills here are lower – around 1,300ft – but equally bare and windswept, but unlike the Dales, covered in heather (see pp 74, 82). Like the Dales, also, the interest in the Moors lies in the major river valleys again called dales. In the north is Eskdale running almost due east from the Cleveland Hills to the sea at Whitby. The remainder run south down what is called the 'dip' slope into the Vale of Pickering in a series of parallel deep narrow vales which, green among the purple hills, have been described as resembling the slashed sleeve of an Elizabethan doublet. Of these rivers, by far the most interesting is the Yorkshire Derwent whose headwaters rise within a hundred yards of the North Sea but prevented by a glacial plug of boulder clay from flowing eastwards, turn south and then westward to flow 60 or more miles to the sea at the head of the Humber Estuary collecting the other Moors' rivers as it flows through the Vale of Pickering.

The Wolds and the cliffs south of Scarborough are part of the arc of chalk that runs up from Dorset through Norfolk and Lincolnshire and juts out into the North Sea at Flamborough Head. The Wolds themselves are remarkably fertile and even the scarp slope is cultivated. As the plethora of fine 'Perpendicular' limestone churches indicates, the East Riding was until the early 19th century devoted to the wool trade and the rearing of sheep, and shared in the great medieval wool boom when wealthy merchants assuaged their consciences by building churches. Nowadays the area is largely devoted to arable farming and the Wolds produce barley, clover, oats and turnips. The lower lands of Holderness – the region between the Wolds and the sea that Winifred Holtby called 'South Riding' – are given over to wheat. This area is composed mainly of 'drift' or glacially deposited sands and clays. This soft material is easily eroded by the sea and Holderness loses about one yard of its shoreline land every year. Villages and towns which once housed thriving communities now lie beneath the sea and, it is said, the bells of drowned churches can be heard amidst the waves on still nights.

The photographs in this book follow an imaginary journey beginning in the southern Pennine district and progressing clockwise through the Dales, across the Vale of York and over the North Yorks Moors to the coast, then down the coast to Flamborough and across the Wolds to Selby. Although on each photograph the current administrative location is given for those who might wish to visit the places shown, the old 'Riding' is also shown in the fond belief that one day Greater Yorkshire will be itself again.

Lindholme, October 1979   *Alan Hollingsworth*

Hebden Bridge near Halifax, West Yorkshire. With its cotton mills, dye works and iron foundries, Hebden Bridge is typical of many of the smaller industrial towns of the West Riding. Set in a deep hollow in the Pennine Moors where Hebden Water – hence the name – joins the River Calder, it has a hard rugged Yorkshire charm in both its architecture and its setting.

8

Leeds Civic Hall, West Yorkshire. Archi-tecture of a different type. Leeds Civic Hall was opened in 1933 by King George V. The twin towers are surmounted by golden owls which form a prominent feature of the city's coat of arms. Inside the banqueting hall commemorates many of Leeds great citizens of the past from Congreve, the Restoration dramatist, to Phil May the cartoonist. Leeds itself is the second city of Yorkshire and the sixth in England.

10

Knaresborough, North Yorkshire (West Riding). Another town in an enchanting natural setting, Knaresborough stands on the summit of a limestone hill and flows down the steep bank of the gorge carved by the River Nidd. Three bridges cross the gorge and the one seen here is the railway viaduct. Visible through the central span are the chequer-board eaves of the Old Manor House, a many gabled and half timbered mansion dating from the 13th century. Inside is preserved the bed upon which Oliver Cromwell slept. But Knaresborough had sad memories for Cromwell. It was in a skirmish outside the town that his son, Oliver, a captain in the Ironsides, was killed.

12

Brimham Rocks near Pately Bridge, North Yorkshire (West Riding). Made of a coarse form of sandstone known as millstone grit, Brimham Rocks have been carved by nature into a series of fantastic shapes which might have been sculpted by giants. Four of them are known as rocking stones and one of these pairs is seen here. Millstone grit – once in demand for millstones as its name implies – tends to weather into natural steps and is much enjoyed by rock climbers. (There is a well-known training face here.) There are also many legends about the rocks themselves. They were once regarded as the work of Druids and some of them carry names like Druid's Altar and Druid's Head. As with almost every crag in the Pennines, there is also the legend of the love-lorn couple who eloped, were pursued and caught on the crag and leapt hand-in-hand into the void preferring death to capture and separation. In the case of the Brimham couple Edwin and Julia however, a safe landing led to parental consent and an eternally happy marriage. Even that could not outlive the legend or their Lovers' Rock.

14

Bolton Abbey, Wharfedale, North Yorkshire (West Riding). Painted by Landseer and Turner and celebrated in verse by Wordsworth, Bolton Priory – to give it a more accurate title – was founded in 1120 by monks of the Order of St Augustine. It was surrendered by the Prior and his canons in January 1538 to King Henry VIII's men at the Dissolution and in 1542 the King sold it to the Earl of Cumberland with all its lands for £2,490 1s 1d. At the time of the Dissolution, the monks were building the western tower which can still be seen in its unfinished state. The nave was preserved for use as the local parish church and is still in use today. Most of the stone from the ruined part of the priory was used by the first owner to transform the gateway into Bolton Hall – a shooting lodge for which purpose the present owner, the Duke of Devonshire, continues to use it.

Barden Bridge, Wharfedale, North Yorkshire (West Riding). Footpaths on either side of the River Wharfe lead to Barden Bridge a mile above the Strid at Bolton Abbey. A 17th century structure now scheduled as an ancient monument, Barden Bridge and the nearby Barden Tower have associations with a local legend of the 'Shepherd Lord' — Lord Henry Clifford. To put the bridge itself in historical perspective — it is said that Dick Whittington himself passed over this same structure on his way to London, fame and fortune from his home at Appletrewick higher up the Dale. Stout Yorkshiremen from these parts have been taking the south by storm ever since.

18

Barden Tower, Wharfedale, North Yorkshire (West Riding). Barden Tower, formerly a small hunting lodge — hunting lodges abound in the Dales — was rebuilt by the 'Shepherd Lord' about 1485. His story takes us back to the Wars of the Roses when his father, known as Butcher Clifford, died fighting for the Red Rose when Edward IV, son of the White Rose Duke of York, came to the throne and Henry and his brother had to be concealed from the King's vengeance. Henry was brought up by a shepherd, was used to walking barefoot in rags and sleeping on straw. After the battle of Bosworth Field and the final triumph of the Lancastrians, he was able to claim his inheritance and take up his seat in the House of Lords where he arrived looking, it was said, like a ploughman. Because he kept his simple ways after regaining his title — he preferred, for example, to live in the peace of Barden Tower rather than in his castle at Skipton — he became known as the Good Lord Clifford. Nonetheless he was enough of his father's son to split his fair share of Scottish skulls at Flodden in 1513 at the head of his personal levy of Craven men. The Tower itself was restored by one of Henry's descendants, Lady Anne Clifford, in 1658 but fell into disuse after her death. The roof was removed in 1777 and the building became derelict.

Burnsall, Wharfedale, North Yorkshire. One of the West Riding's many attractive villages, Burnsall stands on the site of an early Saxon, possibly a Viking, settlement and its 12th century church contains a Norse-Danish font and there are also some Norse hogs-back gravestones. Since the days of the first Queen Elizabeth Burnsall has been noted for the annual sports that are held on the village green to mark the feast of St Wilfred of Ripon, the Church's patron saint. This remains an event of more than local importance since among traditional country sports is the celebrated classic Fell Race which attracts athletes from all over the country.

22

Linton in Craven, Wharfedale, North York-shire (West Riding). Linton Beck, a tribu-tary of the Wharfe, divides the Green and is crossed not only by this very attractive packhorse bridge but by a clapper bridge, a modern road bridge, stepping stones and a ford. The imposing building in the back-ground is not the Town Hall but a 'hospital' founded and endowed for indigent women in 1721 by Richard Fountaine, another Yorkshireman who made good in London. (He gives his name to the local inn.) The hospital comprises seven almshouses and was enlarged in the 19th century.

Landscape near Cray, Wharfedale, North Yorkshire (West Riding). Cray is on the road between Buckden and Aysgarth in the very heart of the Dales at the point where Wharfedale becomes Langstrothdale .On the left is the terraced slope of Buckden Pike which rises to 2,302ft. The word 'cray' means 'fresh and clean' from the language we now call Welsh but which the ancient Britons once used hereabouts.

26

Kilnsey Crag, Wharfedale, North Yorkshire (West Riding). One of the most outstanding landmarks in upper Wharfedale, Kilnsey Crag is a typical outcrop of the carboniferous limestone found in this part of Yorkshire, a hard rock in a hard county! The crag's beetling brow — undercut by the glaciers of the last ice age — has long been a challenge to climbers and it was first conquered in 1957. Below the crag, down towards the river, are level pastures where the local agricultural society holds its annual show and sports, including, of course, the Crag Race. Young men of the district race up to the highest point of the crag and back to the show ground. Older men keep a note of performance and times to make sure the breed isn't getting soft.

28

Arncliffe, Littondale, North Yorkshire (West Riding). Littondale — its old name was 'Amerdale' — is watered by the River Skirfare which flows into the Wharfe near Kilnsey and is a craggy mountain valley shaped by glacial action. Arncliffe is its 'capital' with an attractive clutch of limestone houses grouped round the village green. It has a long history — a bell in the church is dated 1350 and alongside memorials to more recent wars is an inscription to 34 men who went to the battle of Flodden Field 400 years earlier. Charles Kingsley was a frequent visitor and wrote part of *The Water Babies* here.

30

Kettlewell, a view from the road to Coverdale, North Yorkshire (West Riding). Sitting
at the foot of Great Whernside (2,310ft)
Kettlewell, which takes its name from
'Ketel' an Irish Norse chief, is a major centre
for walkers and climbers and potholers in
the Dales. The road from which this photograph was taken climbs up from the village
in the Wharfe valley to about 1,600ft over
the top and then descends into Coverdale,
which runs down into the Ure valley known
32   as Wensleydale.

Langstrothdale, looking towards Hubberholme, North Yorkshire (West Riding). Up the Wharfe valley from Buckden to the source of the river where two becks flow together at Beckermonds was once a game and deer preserve called Langstroth Chase — 'long marsh' Chase now known as Langstrothdale. This photograph, taken in mid-winter looking across Hubberholme to the slopes of Buckden Pike, conveys the bleak grandeur of Yorkshire's highest fells.

34

Pen-y-ghent from Horton in Ribblesdale, North Yorkshire (West Riding). A Welsh mountain in the heart of Yorkshire Dales — the name means a hill of the border country or perhaps, and more credibly, 'a hill of open country' — it is a reminder too that Welsh was the tongue of the Ancient Britons. Pen-y-ghent is one of a group of mountains making up the Craven Uplands, and of three parallel summits: Great Whernside (2,310ft) in the west, Ingleborough (2,373ft) in the middle and Pen-y-ghent (2,273ft) in the east. Formed from a fold in the Earth's crust, these mountains have been cut through by the various rivers that give their names to the Dales — Wharfe, Litton, and Ribble. As is clear in the photograph the various layers of rock can be picked out — particularly noticeable here is the carboniferous limestone girdling the mountain. Among other things, the limestone is riddled with caves and on the slopes of Pen-y-ghent are such famous potholes as Hull Pot and Hunt Pot.

Park Fell and Ingleborough seen from Ribble Head, North Yorkshire (West Riding). Park Fell (1,836ft) is the northern spur of a mountain ridge of which Ingleborough (2,373ft) is the major peak; Simon Fell (2,088ft) is to the east and not seen here. Ingleborough has a millstone cap almost a mile in circumference which has been used as a racecourse. Two of the caves in the flanks of Ingleborough — White Scar cave on the west and Ingleborough cave on the south-west — are famed for their displays of stalactites and stalagmites.

38

Landscape near Stainforth, North Yorkshire (West Riding). Although limestone is soluble in weak acids – of which rainwater is one – carboniferous limestone is not so readily dissolved as the jurassic limestone of the 'Wold' belt that stretches from Dorset to Yorkshire. The result is a harder landscape with frequent outcrops of bare rock deeply fissured by running water. Limestone soils are usually thin and because of this and the porous rock underneath them, they are dry and well-drained. Ash is the most frequent type of woodland on carboniferous limestone of this area.

Malham Cove, North Yorkshire (West Riding). One of Yorkshire's greatest and most spectacular natural features, Malham Cove is a natural amphitheatre of solid limestone, 300ft high. It stands astride the celebrated Pennine Way as it meanders its 250 miles from Edale in Derbyshire to Yetholm over the border in Scotland. At the base of the Cove the infant River Aire, one of Yorkshire's major waterways, emerges from an underground stream to begin its journey down the dale that bears its name, through the great Bradford-Leeds conurbation to Castleford where it joins the Calder – 'Castleford lasses must needs be fair, for they bathe in Calder and wash in Aire'.

Ingleton, North Yorkshire (West Riding). Two small rivers or becks, the Twiss and the Doe converge on Ingleton and flow together to become the River Greta. Both have deep rock-strewn gorges and a series of spectacular waterfalls with a series of intriguing names from Hollybush Spout – most waterfalls are 'Forces' or 'Spouts' in this part of Yorkshire – to Cat Leap Falls. The curious thing about both of these delightful valleys is that they were virtually unknown until the latter half of the last century when the railway reached Ingleton.

44

Buttertubs Pass, Buttertubs, North Yorkshire (North Riding). This intriguingly named pass joins the head of Wensleydale to that of the remoter Swaledale. It gets its name from a group of deep holes in the limestone like the ones depicted here — potholes, 60ft deep and shaped and fluted like an old fashioned butter-tub. The road through the pass joins the two isolated villages of Hawes and Muker. Limestone formations like this — known variously as 'gills', 'pavements' and 'scars' depending upon their shape — abound in the Dales. The rock surfaces are usually devoid of vegetation but the fissures in the rock contain a rich variety of flora, some rare like the Jacob's Ladder of Malham.

Wain Wath Falls near Keld, Upper Swaledale North Yorkshire (North Riding). Typical scenery of a limestone 'gill' or 'scar' — ash trees on the thin soil above the cliff face, a scrub of ash, elm and yew at its base, the river that made the gorge cascading over a limestone step. Wain Wath Falls are just off the road joining Keld to Hoggarths. Keld itself is on the Pennine Way and its name is Old Norse for a spring or well. It was at one time known as 'Appletreekeld.'

River Swale near Gunnerside, Swaledale, North Yorkshire (North Riding). Gunnerside takes its name from yet another ancient Norse chieftain who settled in these parts. The Swale is joined here by Gunnerside Beck which runs through a deep defile on the flanks of Rogan's Seat — a wild trackless and almost untrodden fell. Ivelet Bridge — not in the picture — is a hump-backed bridge in the village said to be haunted by the ghost of *a headless dog*! Across the valley we also find the aptly named village of Crackpot.

50

Bainbridge, Wensleydale, North Yorkshire (North Riding). In Norman times Bainbridge was an important outpost in the great Forest of Wensleydale and boasted no less than 12 foresters. The forest has now disappeared but the custom of blowing a horn at 10 o'clock each winter evening to guide be-nighted travellers to the town still prevails. The white building in the picture is the 'Rose and Crown' which goes back more than 500 years. Near it on the Green is the village's only 'church' — a Quaker Meeting House where George Fox once preached.

Aysgarth Force, Wensleydale, North Yorkshire (North Riding). A sight that inspired the greatest of English 19th century artists – J. M. W. Turner – is the cascade of the waters of the River Ure down what are literally three flights of steps making up Aysgarth Force.

54

Castle Bolton, Wensleydale, North Yorkshire (North Riding). Not to be confused with Bolton Abbey further south in Wharfedale, Castle Bolton was built by Richard de Scrope round about 1386 to defend Wensleydale against the depredations of marauding bands of Scots from over the border. It represents a late flowering of the castle building art — not so much a castle more a fortified house with a balance between the claims of defence and the comfort and domestic felicity of the occupants. Externally grim and forbidding, the castle has strongly built towers, each with a porticullis and window openings of negligible size. Internally, all its rooms faced into a courtyard with large windows. Mary Queen of Scots was held prisoner here for six months in 1568. Later during the Civil War it was held for the King by Colonel Chaytor and withstood a prolonged siege which only ended — on 5 November 1645 — when all the horses had been eaten. In more recent times it was the site chosen by the television producers of *All Creatures Great and Small* for James Herriot to propose to his Helen.

East Witton, near Middleham, North Yorkshire (North Riding). Once a thriving market town with a charter dating back to 1309, East Witton now largely comprises this picturesque elongated village green with its attractive but standard cottages. The village was rebuilt in 1908 by the Earl of Ailesbury.

West Tanfield, North Yorkshire (North Riding). A glimpse through the span of the 18th century bridge over the River Ure of one of the most enchanting villages of North Yorkshire. As Nicholaus Pevsner puts it, 'the church tower and the castle gatehouse just avoid looking at one another'. The church is St Nicolas' and parts of it date back to c1200. It is full of tombs and memorials to the Marmions who came to the village in 1215 and later built the castle of which only the gatehouse now remains. One of its attractive features is the oriel window overlooking the bridge and the river.

60

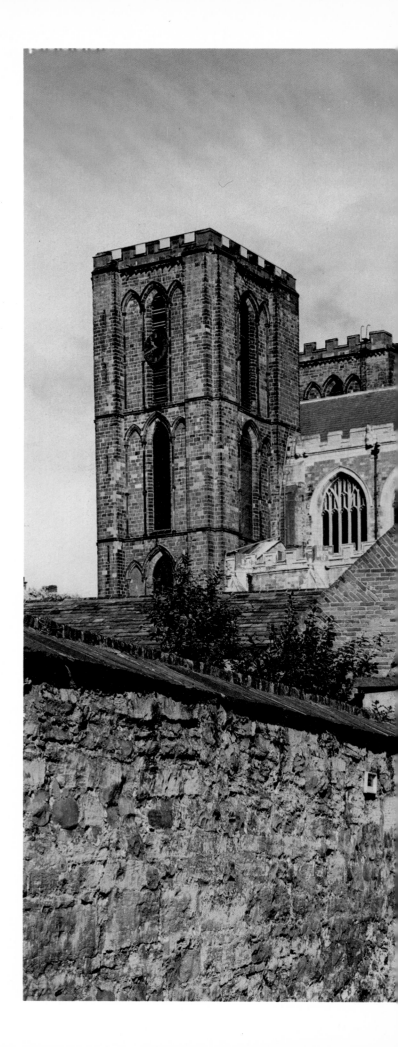

Ripon Cathedral, North Yorkshire (West Riding). Almost certainly one of the oldest Christian buildings in the British Isles, Richmond Cathedral crypt is said to have been built about 670AD for St Wilfrid, Bishop of York, who founded a monastery here on the site of a wooden structure believed to have been built in 657 by the Abbot of Melrose. The monastery was subsequently destroyed and rebuilt in the 12th century. Additions and alterations were made over the centuries – the Gothic nave dates from 1502 – and there was the inevitable Victorian restoration when Sir G. Gilbert Scott was the architect. The towers originally had spires but the last was removed in 1664.

Byland Abbey, Coxwold, North Yorkshire (North Riding). In 1134 Abbot Gerold and 12 of his monks from Calder in Cumberland set out to found a new Cistercian monastery and after wandering for 43 years settled here after three other false starts. They laid the foundations of a splendid abbey which once boasted the biggest church of the Cistercian order in England. The picture shows the major remnant of that church, the west wall. The beautiful doorway has a 13th century style trefoil head with rich mouldings and above it are three superb lancet windows with blind arcading between them. Above these is the lower half of the frame of a rose window, 26ft in diameter. At Coxwold itself, Laurence Sterne, author of *Tristram Shandy* and *The Sentimental Journey* was the incumbent from 1761 for the last eight years of his life. He gave his house the name of Shandy Hall. There is also a legend that Oliver Cromwell's headless body is buried at Newburgh Priory. (His head, of course, turns up from time to time in Auction Rooms)

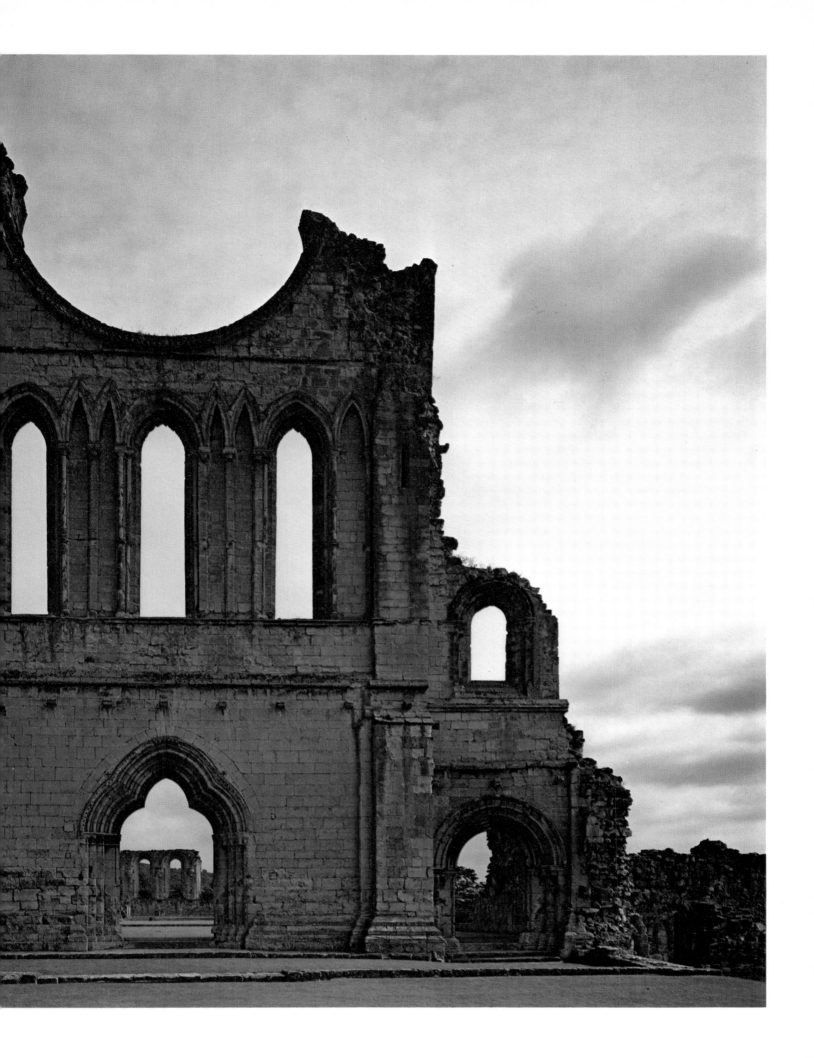

Helmsley, North Yorkshire. This charming little North Riding market town sits at the head of what, in geological time was the great glacial 'melt-water', 'Lake Pickering'. It boasts a fine church visible in the background of the picture that looks old but is in fact a 19th century 'restoration' in 13th century style retaining some parts of an earlier church including a fine Norman south doorway. There is also a castle, founded in the 12th century and 'slighted' after a three months' siege during the Civil War. Helmsley also marks the start of the Cleveland Way which, opened in 1969, follows the perimeter of the North York Moors in a great sweep northwards, then eastwards, then southwards through Whitby and down the coast to Filey 100 miles in all following the footsteps of the Roman legions, medieval monks and drovers and seamen in more recent times along the top of the North Sea cliffs.

Rievaulx Abbey, near Helmsley, North Yorkshire (North Riding). The first Cistercian abbey in Yorkshire, Rievaulx — the name means 'the valley of the Rye' or Ryedale — was founded in 1131 by Walter Espece, Lord of Helmsley. The Cistercians were an austere and hard-working order — at least in the early days of their history — with a deep interest in agriculture and 'Gothic' architecture. The first settlers at Rievaulx would have found the site covered in thick scrub forest, prickly with hawthorn and brambles and infested with wolves and wildcats. Over the centuries, they not only cleared the site and built their magnificent abbey, but they also developed the pasturage on the Yorkshire uplands and became wealthy (and a good deal less austere) on the wool trade. They set up a thriving iron industry and they built water-mills, windmills and bridges all over the area. Their industry virtually changed the face of the north-east of Yorkshire — there were sister foundations like Fountains, Bylands and Jervaulx and many smaller houses in the foot hills of the moors like Baysdale and Rosedale. Although the abbey was dissolved by Henry VIII in 1539, its remains are among the most complete in the country and have been carefully preserved by the Ministry of the Environment for over 50 years.

68

Lastingham, North Yorkshire (North Riding). Nestling under the slopes of Spaunton Moor with the delightfully named Camomile Hill looking over it, Lastingham occupies a peaceful site that has attracted mankind since the earliest times. Nearby are traces of settlements by Brigantes, a powerful tribe of Ancient Britons, of Romans who drove them out and of the Saxons who gave the village its name. Of particular interest is the church of St Mary's which was an 11th century crypt which Nicholaus Pevsner describes as 'unforgettable'. It is believed to have been built over the grave of St Cedd who founded a monastery hereabouts in 660 AD.

Northdale Beck, Rosedale Abbey, North Yorkshire (North Riding). Northdale Beck is a tributary of the River Seven which is the main stream of Rosedale. This area was once highly forested and in Tudor times the ready availability of charcoal and the remoteness of the area attracted a group of French glass makers to flout the then government monopoly. Many prospered and some of the large houses they built are still to be seen. There are also the remains of coal-pits and iron workings. This end of Rosedale is also renowned for the prevalence of thunderstorms — the reason perhaps for the name Thorgill across the valley from where this photograph was taken. Some authorities suggest that the presence of ironstone outcrops may attract the thunder but the reason is more likely to be that the North Yorkshire Moors rise quite sharply some 1,500ft down the prevailing wind from the essentially flat Vale of York and create the storms by what meteorologists call 'orographic effect.'

Rosedale Moor, North Yorkshire (North Riding). This is grouse moor country and there is a shooting butt made of turf and stones in the centre of the picture. The red grouse is a characteristic moorland bird and one which is unique to the British Isles. It feeds mainly upon the young shoots of heather and, being a ground nesting bird, it depends upon the density of the heather allied to its own protective colouring to survive the attentions of a host of predators. It is a common practice on grouse moors to burn off the older heather to ensure an abundant supply of young shoots and to destroy the eggs and larvae of parasites.

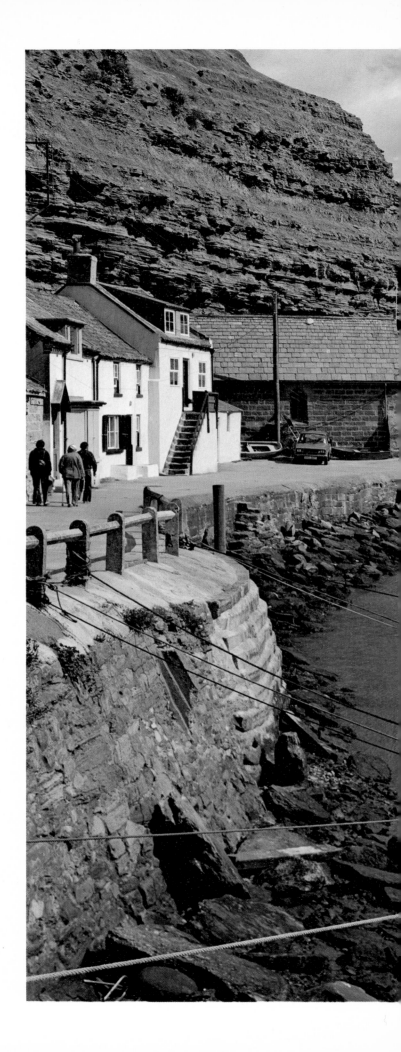

Staithes, North Yorkshire (North Riding). Roxby Beck swirling down from Roxby High Moor has cut a deep creek through precipitous cliffs to the sea and Staithes, a pretty fishing port, has been built on either side of the 'grove'. To the north is Cowbar Nab a menacing vertical sandstone cliff visible in the left background. Captain Cook the great explorer served his apprenticeship here to a local grocer and draper until he ran away to sea at Whitby to find a continent, fame and fortune and, eventually, a martyr's death. 'Staithes' means a jetty or landing place.

The Sands, Whitby, North Yorkshire (North Riding). This picture taken looking north-west into the summer sunset shows the full extent of Whitby's famous Sands running three miles from the West Pier to the appropriately named Sandsend, just visible here. The building on the cliff top is the golf course club house.

78

Whitby Abbey, Whitby, North Yorkshire (North Riding). Following an epic battle of the Saxon 7th century when Christian King Oswy defeated and killed the pagan King Penda of Mercia, Oswy made a vow which led to the foundation on this site of a monastery for both men and women in 657. The first abbess was St Hilda who, legend has it, cleared the area of snakes. The original abbey was sacked by the Danes in 867 and only a few remnants of the Saxon building remain. The present ruins belong to the monastery as it was refounded in c1067 and the main surviving part – the abbey church whose west front is seen here – dates from the 13th and 14th centuries. It was here also that Caedmon, a humble swineherd, dreamed his dream and in writing his *Song of Creation* became the first poet in the language. He felt as many have felt since on this hallowed site:

'Now we must praise the Guardian of Heaven's realm, The Creator's might and His mind's thought'.

Egton High Moor and Fylingdales Early Warning Station, North Yorkshire (North Riding). What Sir Nicholaus Pevsner calls 'The geometry of the space age at its most alluring and most frightening'. the Fylingdales Early Warning Station is designed to maintain vigilance against a surprise missile attack upon the free world from the Soviet Union. As seen here it is an eerie presence in a desolate moorland setting. More reassuring perhaps is the homely heather in the foreground – calluna vulgaris – which abounds on the Yorkshire Moors to the delight of the bees and the benefit of the grouse. It is notoriously difficult to photograph.

This standard gauge railway which runs 18 miles from Pickering through the awe-inspiring ice age geology of Newtondale and across Goathland and Egton High Moors to Grosmont, is rather more than just a steam preservation project. It is in fact a fully operational National Park rail service making a major contribution to the life and welfare of a scattered rural community. Founded in 1972, the railway operates both steam and diesel locomotives — the train in the picture is drawn by GNR 0-6-0ST No 1247 — and carries more than a quarter of a million passengers a year.

84

Hole of Horcum, Saltesgate, North Yorkshire (North Riding). A mythical giant Wada or Wade is reputed to have dug this natural amphitheatre with his bare hands and flung the fistfulls of soil to make the nearby rounded hilltop of Blakey Topping. It is also credited to the Devil as one of his many punchbowls. It is more likely to have been created by another giant – the glacial ice of the last ice age and still lurking in its cool depths are ferns found elsewhere only in the Arctic.

Castle Howard, North Yorkshire (North Riding). What you could buy for £78,250 in 1737! Vanbrugh the poet and dramatist who was later to design Blenheim Palace for the Duke of Marlborough, made the drawings for Castle Howard at the request of the third Earl of Carlisle (family name Howard) in 1699. Vanbrugh, talented amateur though he was, was wise enough to employ Nicholas Hawksmoor as his clerk of works as that other talented amateur – Christopher Wren – had done before him. Building began in 1701 and was still in progress when Vanbrugh died in 1726. This photograph is taken across the North Lake with the Great Hall with its dome just visible over the trees. To the left is the Kitchen Court, a rather austere building with four towers.

Hovingham, North Yorkshire (North Riding). A gem of a village in the vale of Pickering on the road from Malton to Helmsley, Hovingham is the family seat of the Worsley family and the home of the Duchess of Kent. The village has been the centre of a flourishing agricultural community for the best part of a thousand years with markets and fairs going back to Saxon times. It was also the site of a major Roman villa with under-floor heating and tassellated floors. The ruins were first discovered in 1745 when Sir Thomas Worsley, Surveyor General and a close friend of George III, built Hovingham Hall and laid out its grounds. Hovingham also boasts a celebrated cricket field on which festival matches are held usually at the time of Scarborough's cricket week.

Scarborough, the Castle, Harbour and old town, North Yorkshire (North Riding). Old Scarborough with its narrow steep streets, many of them flights of steps, and dominated by the Castle Rock has been likened to Gibraltar. Before the discovery of 'Spaw' waters in the late 18th century and the burgeoning popularity of 'watering places' in the 19th had begun the development of Yorkshire's premier seaside resort, Scarborough was an important haven and centre for both fishing and the Baltic trade. The castle itself was built in the 12th century and was used by, among others, King John and Edward I. It was the scene of a rebellion in Mary Tudor's reign and was besieged twice in the Civil War finally surrendering to the Parliamentarians in 1645 when it was mined and partly destroyed. It was also damaged by German shellfire during World War I. As can be seen in the picture, the Harbour has three piers. The oldest is the Old Pier — the landward end of the pier in the centre — which dates back 700 years. Its seaward extension is Vincent's Pier which has the lighthouse on it and was added after 1732. The East and West piers date from the early 19th century.

Bempton Cliffs, near Flamborough Head, (East Riding). These precipitous cliffs are now on the southern border of North Yorkshire where the ancient county becomes the recently created North Humberside. They mark the northern end of the great chalk escarpment that runs diagonally across England from Dorset through Norfolk and Lincolnshire to the Yorkshire Wolds and the North Sea. The soft inaccessible rocks provide nesting sites for thousands of sea birds.

94

The Wolds near Duggleby, North Yorkshire (East Riding). These smooth rounded low chalk uplands with their well drained soil and comparatively warm dry climate are first class arable farmland and highly productive of both wheat and barley — and from the picture, that inevitable accompaniment to roast beef and Yorkshire pudding — Brussels Sprouts.

96

The Wolds near East Lutton, North Yorkshire (East Riding). The rolling rounded hills of typical chalk 'downland' that comprise the Yorkshire Wolds. Until the early 19th century they were devoted to grass and the rearing of sheep. Pioneering farming methods introduced a new farming system that grew fodder for sheep and now the area has an exceptionally high proportion of arable land given over to turnips, oats clover and as evident here, barley.

Flamborough Head, North Humberside. This forbidding chalk headland towering 150ft above the North Sea shows with its proliferation of caves and arches the effects of the battering it has received over the centuries. Flamborough also gives its name to a memorable sea fight between ships of the Royal Navy and a force of American warships under the command of John Paul Jones in 1779. HMS *Seraphis* surrendered when sinking and Jones's ship, the *Bonhomme Richard* sank next day. There is a memorial plaque near the lighthouse and the anchor of Jones' ship can be seen in St Nicholas Gardens in Scarborough. John Paul Jones himself is entombed in the crypt of the US Naval Academy at Annapolis, Maryland and his words as he was called upon to surrender early in the battle are immortal – '*I have not yet begun to fight*'.

York, City walls and Minster. Two of York's most interesting architectural and historical attractions, are the city walls and the Minster. The Romans first walled the city when they set up a legionary fortress in 71 AD; the city was destroyed by fire in 1069 and the Normans built a new walled fortress between 1250 and 1300. Inside the walls were crammed 40 churches, nine chapels, four monasteries and four friaries as well as 16 hospitals and nine guildhalls — which serves to explain the narrowness of the streets and the density of the buildings in the centre of the city even today. The walls were restored during the 19th century and became a public pathway. York Minster is the largest Gothic church in England and dates from the 13th century but its origins go back to a tiny church on the site which was established when the mission of St Augustine came to convert England to Christianity in 597.

Selby Abbey Church, North Yorkshire (West Riding). Originally built as a monastery church to serve a Benedictine community established here in 1097, Selby Abbey church survived the Dissolution of the Monasteries and became the parish church of this fascinating shipbuilding port on the River Ouse. The Abbey Church has fine Norman doorways — the west door can be seen in the picture — and many features illustrating the development of church architecture from the Norman to the Early English styles. Fire destroyed the roof of the tower in 1906 but it was skilfully restored in 1909.

A farm in upper Teesdale, Durham (North Riding). A winter's scene that is at once a reminder that the latitude of this northern extremity of traditional Yorkshire is that of Moscow and Edmonton and that in these high fells life is hard for both man and beast.

High Force Waterfall, Teesdale, Durham (North Riding). At this point on its 70-mile journey from Cross Fell in Cumbria to the North Sea near Middlesbrough, the River Tees negotiates an exposed section of the Whin Sill and falls 50ft into a deep swirling cauldron. The Whin Sill itself is an intrusion of hard dolerite rocks into the softer limestone and which further north the Romans used as the base of part of Hadrian's Wall.

Farmhouse near Newbiggin, Teesdale, Cumbria (North Riding). Most of the farm buildings, drystone walls and roadways are built of local stone in Teesdale — a sandstone called millstone grit. There is a quarry at Egglestone a few miles from where this photograph was taken producing an appropriately named 'Windy Hill' building stone.

110

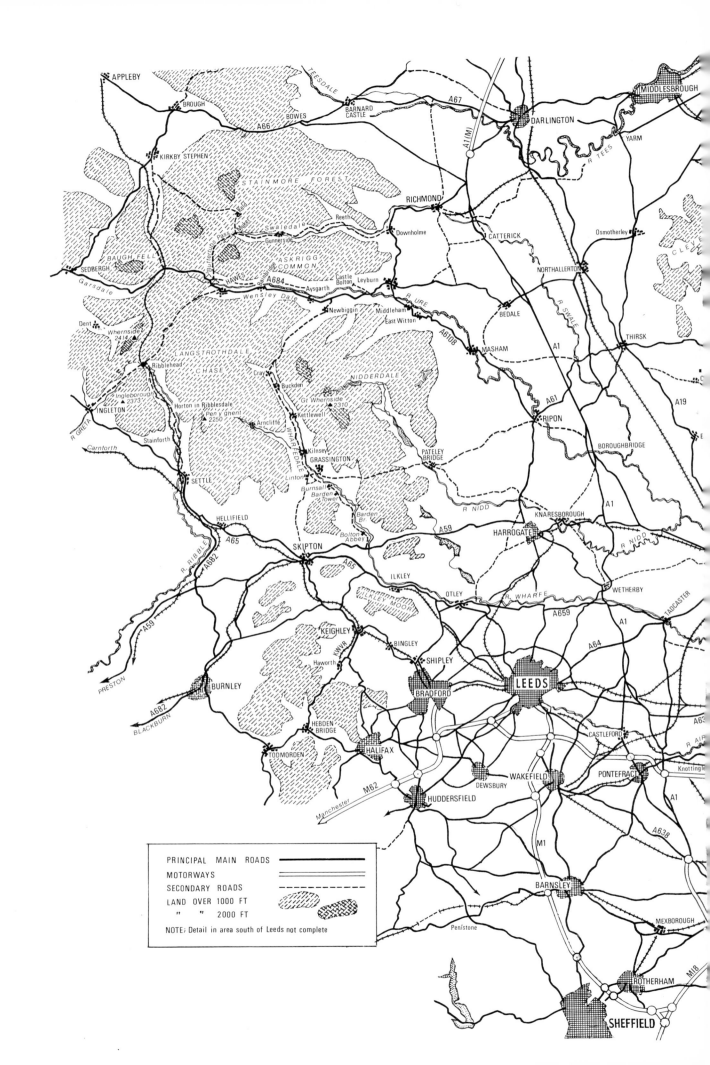

APPLEBY
BROUGH
BOWES
BARNARD CASTLE
A66
TEESDALE
A67
MIDDLESBROUGH
DARLINGTON
A1(M)
R TEES
YARM

KIRKBY STEPHEN

STAINMORE FOREST
Reeth
RICHMOND
Reeth
Swaledale
Muker
Gunnerside
Downholme
CATTERICK
Osmotherley
CLEVE

BAUGH FELL
Garsdale
SEDBERGH
ASKRIGG COMMON
A684
HAWES
Aysgarth
Castle Bolton
Leyburn
NORTHALLERTON

Wensley Dale
Newbiggin
Middleham
East Witton
R URE
BEDALE
R SWALE
THIRSK

Dent
Whernside
2414
LANGSTROTHDALE CHASE
Cray
Buckden
NIDDERDALE
A6108
MASHAM
A1
A19

Ribblehead
Ingleborough
2373
Horton in Ribblesdale
Pen y ghent
2250
Arncliffe
Gt Whernside
2310
Kettlewell
A61
RIPON

INGLETON
R GRETA
Carnforth
Stainforth
Kilnsey
GRASSINGTON
Linton
PATELEY BRIDGE
BOROUGHBRIDGE

SETTLE
Burnsall
Barden Tower
WHARFEDALE
R NIDD
KNARESBOROUGH
A1

HELLIFIELD
Barden Br.
A59
HARROGATE
R NIDD

R RIBBLE
A65
A682
SKIPTON
Bolton Abbey
A59

A65
ILKLEY
OTLEY
R. WHARFE
WETHERBY
TADCASTER

A59
ILKLEY MOOR
A659
A1
PRESTON
A64

KEIGHLEY
BINGLEY
SHIPLEY
LEEDS

Haworth
KWVR
BRADFORD
CASTLEFORD
A63

BURNLEY
R AIRE

A682
HEBDEN BRIDGE
WAKEFIELD
PONTEFRACT
Knottingley

BLACKBURN
TODMORDEN
HALIFAX
DEWSBURY
A1

M62
HUDDERSFIELD
M1
A638

Manchester

PRINCIPAL MAIN ROADS
MOTORWAYS
SECONDARY ROADS
LAND OVER 1000 FT
" " 2000 FT

NOTE: Detail in area south of Leeds not complete

BARNSLEY

Peniston e
MEXBOROUGH

M18

ROTHERHAM

SHEFFIELD